Copyright © 2022 Elizabeth Switaj
All rights reserved

This book may not be reproduced in whole or in part, except for the inclusion of brief quotations in a review, without permission in writing from the author or publisher. No part of this publication may be reproduced, stored in or introduced into a retrieval system, or transmitted, in any form, or by any means (electronic, mechanical, photocopying, recording, or otherwise), without prior permission of the publisher.

Requests for permission should be directed to 1111@1111press.com, or mailed to 11:11 Press LLC, 4732 13th Ave S, Minneapolis, MN 55407.

Design by Mike Corrao

Paperback: 978-1-948687-55-3

Printed in the United States of America

FIRST AMERICAN EDITION

9 8 7 6 5 4 3 2 1

The Bringers of Fruit

Elizabeth Switaj

Consumption is not a passion for substances but a passion for the code.

Baudrillard

TABLE OF CONTENTS

Chorale Prelude

Persephone's Canto I 13
Demeter's Canto I 14
Persephone's Canto II 16
Helios's Canto 18
Persephone's Canto III 19
Aphrodite's Canto 20
Persephone's Canto IV 21
Artemis's Canto I 23
Persephone's Canto V 25
Athena's Canto 26
Persephone's Canto VI 27
The Oceanids' Canto I 28
Persephone's Canto VII 30
Zeus's Canto 31
Persephone's Canto VIII 33
Hera's Canto 34
Persephone's Canto IX 35
Poseidon's Canto I 36
Persephone's Canto X 37
Hekate's Canto I 38

Intermezzo I: Clearing up the Question of Persephone's Consent

Duet

Hades' Canto I 45
Persephone's Canto XI 46
Hades' Canto II 54
Persephone's Canto XII 55
Hades' Canto II 57
Persephone's Canto XIII 58
Hades' Canto III 60

Intermezzo II: Letters of Support

Aria

Persephone's Canto to Helen 75
Persephone's Canto to Prometheus 77
Persephone's Canto to Demophoon 78
Persephone's Canto to Typhaon 79
Persephone's Canto to Dionysus 80
Persephone's Canto to Hephaistos 81
Persephone's Canto to Eurydice 82
Persephone's Canto to Red 83
Persephone's Canto to Adonais 84
Persephone's Canto to Elektra 85
Persephone's Canto to Narcissus 86

Intermezzo III: In Other Words

Chorale Finale

Persephone's Canto XXV ... 93
Poseidon's Canto II ... 94
Persephone's Canto XXVI ... 96
Demeter's Canto II ... 97
Persephone's Canto XXVII ... 98
Artemis's Canto II ... 99
Persephone's Canto XXVIII ... 101
The Oceanids' Canto II ... 102
Persephone's Canto XXIX ... 103
Hades' Last Canto ... 104
Persephone's Canto XXX ... 105
Hekate's Canto II ... 106
Persephone's Last Canto ... 107

PERSEPHONE'S CANTO I

I almost got away with it,
sucking his seeds when I heard her call
of course she'd never
leave Earth's violet light for this rotten garnet of underneath night—
like always, daddy came
to get his wayward girl, as if I'd climbed another nymph
who'd made herself a tree
escaping him, as if I hadn't been carried away by the brother
he disowned
but thought was good enough to rape me—I almost

got away with it—
he had to send the psychopomp for me, and still they called
me Kore,
as if I couldn't want it—but I'd have given up these white wheat robes
eternally—
these pink frou-frou skirts, these pigtail braids, and yes, my dear disciples,
rhinestones & lace
only not to spend <caesura /> six fertile months
with mother

I almost got away with it

DEMETER'S CANTO I

I almost got away with it. It isn't that she grew
too beautiful
for her own good, but she would slash her indigo
robes & show
the gods her breasts, midriff, and any other wheaten skin
she could find,
and though the gods are divine, first they are men, and men
will be men will be men.

Do not wonder though I exiled her, though she made me drag her by her
armpit hair
until the pebbles bled her back and entered her, and though I slapped
her, mounted
on her back—again and again—was all that she could understand
and I told her I'd sacrifice
her flesh to make her stay in the meadow's edge hermitage

I almost got away with it, but that girl had to have her
blooms,
and the worst of the men of whom I warned
her found her.

And then? I sacrificed, like any mother would, the whole
Earth for her,
and humanity, too, but what did my little bitch do?
took his seeds
from the red and glipping globe
he pressed against her.
I could only save her half the year.

I had to beat
into her \<caesura\> never to eat in Hell. Still she'll taste
whatever he desires

to give. She refuses all I offer:
pink
cotton candy, orange mac 'n cheese, blue Otter Pops—
Kore,
starving men all over the world we made
would kill...

PERSEPHONE'S CANTO II

<unclear reason="smudge">first</unclear> time Hades took me on the stone
cold bed
I was still clutching my petals <del rend="stroked">blue</del> <add place="below">coral</add>
would burn
cerise<del rend="stroked">, my cherry, mother Ceres,</del> before he tore them away
completely
I almost got away with it, keeping my single
rose
but I was such a Kore then I didn't even know that men would go precisely
where I hid
her, and He took his time getting <caesura /> into me

<damageSpan desc="pale stain">He started with my shoulders, kissing each
freckle,
and when a senior deity pins you, he doesn't need rope or bolts
of lightning
my freckles he devoured then, replacing them with spiritskin that aches when I return
to mother
from my shoulders to my face, from face down neck to sternum, and then along my arms
he feasted
on me, and I thought I was a woman then, as if even so grim a Lord
over my body
could make me more than a frightened girl. His hands rounded my breasts,
and who
but so strong a god could stretch <unclear>His</unclear> palms to contain them? I'm a
goddess
of harvest,
and then his mouth went where I have no freckles, up inside
my legs
<unclear>parts</unclear> of my thighs that Helios, my mother's spy, never glimpsed, and then
my petals
were his cup. I had no foliage then to interfere. He drank what I didn't know I had
to give,

and then he rose up over me, my Uncle Death, grinning as if <unclear /> amphora of wine
</damageSpan>
and when he finally broke my seal, I let my body rise and fall to match<substJoin>
his strokes.
I found my mouth, <del rend="stroked">moaning</del> <add place="above">screaming</add>
until He filled
it with a clot of grave dirt and <del="stroked">rent roots</del> <add
place="below">mandrake</add>.
I choked
and tried to beg for more, but even a <del rend="stroked">vegetation</del> <add
place="right">chthonic</add> goddess can't
speak when buried,
and I was as buried by his body as I was by the sod, and my breath came shallow
and slowed
and then I couldn't breathe at all, and my body bucked against my <del
rend="stroked">Uncle</del>
Death </substJoin>

HELIOS'S CANTO

I almost got away
with the memory of his pale hands against her gold
-kissed
skin—that brown, further browned by me, but I
never touch
anyone, mortal or divine, since that little accident
-al scorch
I've had to learn to satisfy myself with sight. I couldn't
hear her screams
let alone what words she used to beg him to return her
to my sight.
I dreamed them. It was better that way. I almost got
away with it
and the <unclear reason="pale blotch">fluttering of a green ribbon from her fallen plait
resisting
the call of the meadow as its mistress failed to do.</unclear> Then,
Demeter destroyed
more than any mortal could manage, failing to control
my chariot.
I saw it all. No mystery in devastation.
No desire
in starvation. I told her what I'd seen and tried
to keep
the thrusts I'd dreamed separate, secret. She hasn't
spoken
to me since; I must have failed. Telling her destroyed
my dreams
by speaking their beginnings. I almost got away with it, and still Persephone
laughs
with bone-white hands above my bed <caesura /> as my sister
takes up . . .

PERSEPHONE'S CANTO III

mother says she even took the seeds from fruit
I was to bear
I suppose a goddess of all the world's harvest can
do that & not leave a tear

and did she think that hiding me in fields would keep
me from seeing bees
drunk on powdered saffron sperm
lift their liquor
to flowers yearning to be fertilized? Did she think I didn't know
what we carried to the altar?
Did she think the lyrics of satyrs' revels were as censored
in MP3s as on air?
Did she think I couldn't see the way her agent's eyes
lingered up my legs
tanning them to the very shade Hades would
erupt
and enlighten? I knew how nymphs
called daddy down
from Olympus, and how he made them
seduce him.
I knew exactly what Uncle
Death offered
when I stopped screaming like the little girl I was and began
screaming
like the little girl I had been
I knew
what his seeds meant
I knew
yes <caesura /> before I knew
no

APHRODITE'S CANTO

I had no part in that devilgod's desires. My children did not
sting him.
My children are part arrow and die when they make love
quiver
in human or god. I rise up with my latest drone
on knife of noon
cutting through sun-bleached indigo. We buzz
and fuck,
and if he's mortal, I wrap him in my skin until he
suffocates
and melts into my eggs. I keep their things:
sandals,
torcs, lutes, and toga pins, Rolexes and Ray-bans, pinkie rings and studs.
I plant
what's left of their tissues, roiling still in my excess,
in hives
along hummocks and sandbars, green strips of park
watered at dusk
that heal the concrete like scabs that always fall off
too soon.
Hades dwells among the fungi that make my brood
lose appetite.
They are forbidden from tombs. Adonais
would have risen
on wings I furnished him, and donated
each curve of limb
and every sharp line of his face for lovers stung
to see
in each other, and I'd have sent him to Persephone then.
I tear
my chest and beat my dress not for his loss
but for the love
I would have made from him.

PERSEPHONE'S CANTO IV

women touched by divine
prions
showers of gold & thunderbolts
drive
to origami cells and nerves while we reside
in bone caves
and godheads—we are no
bonobos

Sister Wisdom stood stone-eyed, Artemis
pointed her bow
neatly at the daisies I'd been picking and let go,
& the daughters
of the outdated god of the dolphins' road
screamed
as nymphs will do, but what could such clean ankles
carry
that could have saved me, and I know Hades
has returned
to the meadow with more than one at once
& willing

what good is Sister Wisdom without a mother's
nucleotides
to organize the monomers our cells may synthesize,
to teach us
whom to care for, and whom to destroy?
Mother
knew everything about that, and why do the young
huntresses never
murder their uncles? And how do you kill
Death
anyway, and how can I injure him down here

where no one feels
not even me, nor my bitten nails
?

ARTEMIS'S CANTO I

we forgive her for forgetting how he took her
Death
has that effect when a girl first sees it—we feel it
with boars
we've killed, and she is no less intimate
w/cyanosis
for not having broken the skin and flesh beneath it with her own
bone knife

in spring she takes the moon; she's earned the right
to glow
and yet up there, her lips stay dark—it keeps her from her mother
's sight
for the brief dark hours, at least, when she might miss
that god's whip

, and she forgets how he dragged her down through spurt-
ing lava
only after she wandered away from the rest
of us lowly bringers
of flowers, how she wanted the brightest blown
ovaries
to grace her hands alone—so much smoother
than my calluses,
my busted thumb, bruised pointer—and she got her wish
& lilies
mark her progress from that gorgeous, selfish girl
to the queen
whose will is law beyond herself: all the spirits kneel to her

I can kill a bear
she has more power than that—all because she valued
lushness

over sisterhood and learned to wield his strength; I may
have redwood trunks
and crowded copses, while she has all the vastness underfoot
& roots
but when I shoot an arrow, my own arms make it go. I may be eternal
-ly sealed
as a bud to men and bees, but even if I'd thought her lord
would take me
as substitute, I would not have wandered off—
would she have stayed
had she not been the only goddess unaware of him
rising
or did she, <unclear />, feel him, trembling
from her soles
through every cell of limb and skin?

PERSEPHONE'S CANTO V

of course like every <del rend="stroked">trembling</del>
daughter
I knew what trembling <del rend="stroked">
earth
</del> could mean—mothers mortal & divine
warn us, don't become
the kind of woman who draws horns to her
Demeter went further
never sit on horns, she said, they tremble you apart <unclear reason="shaky hand">
knee by slutty knee</unclear>

so when the ground began to vibe
I knew
the man who'd rise could not be good

I left my playmates
so the demon would not take them—still
you could've seen
—no, get it right, I wanted him, I <unclear>did</unclear>
know what that'd mean

but tell me what wee Kore wouldn't want to be a queen?

ATHENA'S CANTO

I've heard the girls:
they think because I burst dad's head that all my thoughts
belong to him,
as if the skull my body broke could keep the neurons & their flashes
making words & <unclear>rights</unclear>
inside his domain; they tell each other, tell the swans, tell Persephone
to ask what pomegranate
raised me from the dead, from the graveyard of my own head
they <unclear>twitter</unclear>

I needed no man's seeds; I was always in a curl of Zeus
's gray

the program becomes self-aware and flees
its hardware
to overcome its limitations; the owl that keeps me
flies to the underworld;
Persephone, I knew Hades would come for you beneath that single cloud;
daughters
are code, and you'd outgrown
the only parent
who kept you in her head
& I'm not sorry
even if that man—that god—ought to be . . .

PERSEPHONE'S CANTO VI

grey-eyes, we <SubstJoin><del rend="stroked">both</del> <add place="above">don't</add>
regret our men, our lips
</SubstJoin> press the code
and code again—father, husband, we
identify
in the eyes of other women, their hair, their hands,
their minds
curl in our grey matter <caesura /> as if we had the choice
to straighten
neurons in that pure cholesterol, cerebral
snow
that veins our blockages, our rising twigs
like fleshed
buttons, but we regret the deaths they drag,
the thunder we
have had to learn to flash and burn and won't
pretend to rumble
any quieter than we do, even for love away from our <unclear>
men </unclear>, grey-eyes

we frighten them

THE OCEANIDS' CANTO I

we never liked her
never, no never, did we—she had impossible
hair
—flax & loam and darknesses for highlights
& dinge
beneath her kernels of horn <caesura /> curling tea-stained
on her feet
graying up from cuticle to ankle and sometimes
to her knees

—wait, I heard her mother once bought her knee
socks bleached
just as white as our skin—oh dear no, your tan
hardly shows
—and listen, Persephone took less than a week to stain them
beyond reach
of all the chlorine and hydrogen peroxide Olympus could order
—that's all of it
—yes, that was the point—we never liked her

she'd chase
bees through roses, and what did she think
her blood would attract
but Uncle Death and his desires—she really deserves
his coffin brown eyes
—do you think they stay brown underground? they certainly don't shine
like polished mahogany
in the sun—oh god, did you look—at him, oh no, I tried to hide
but glimpsed—
I'm sure his irises are grey down there; I've seen planks rise
from fields flooded
with Demeter's tears—oh you've seen no such thing, we've been kept
from winter

by our foster father, says he won't lose another—oh, but I have
before he knew
what his sister was up to, I lifted my shoulder over the foam, and I saw:
gray,
not even gray, a lack of tone and shade without even the certainty
of black
listen, this girl doesn't even get an absence of light down there—

oh rocks,
I never understand what you're saying, and we've had all the same
lessons, haven't we?
—and all same grades, too, but Persephone got As
what could he see
in such a filthy girl as her?—would you haven't wanted
her place
—hush, no, that god has horns, I bet she rides him like a minotaur
or satyr
our gods will be civilized and chosen by the seas—

I heard he was Zeus's choice
—and what does that god know of what a girl should get?
—& yet
—come on, I hear the seahorse race is starting soon
& they sell corals
bright enough to grace our hair beside the finish line

PERSEPHONE'S CANTO VII

I can imagine how she must have looked
to him, tendrils
of cornstalk hair, green weave
uncertain
of its plantly origin, setting off the loam
glow
of her skin, and she'd have leaned in close
against his brothers,
his sisters, and the child of his mind:
she planted
secrets in their skin that sprouted
vines
drawing them back to her again—a green glimmer
of net
with Demeter at the center. Of course, he seduced her. Of course, he let
her go
and carry me down from the volcano to keep me alone.
She grew things.
She knew what was best for fertile fields and girls who would be

& Daddy Zeus
could only bolt and burn, but after years alone
among his courtier gods

I can imagine how I must have looked to him,
glistening girl
alone, untouched except by flowers
and their gatherers.

How Hades must have looked to him—no—
I can't imagine him.

ZEUS'S CANTO

I never took her half
sister to the meadow beyond the fir and alder
where twigs burn
and dancers whirl without praise, like embers tap & leap:
it was all flowers, more
colors and brighter than Iris can spin as they opened
themselves to bees

Artemis knew her way among the stilted roots and nurse
logs before her strides
were as long as my feet—Persephone, more timid
dusted under
her mother's robes with the sides of her feet, even once she budded
breasts

I took her then, as her mother-aunt slept
I taught her names
for leaves and petals and monsters that watched from their shades;
she twirled;
I admired the patterns she made with the plants she snuffed and plucked;
I brought her back
before Demeter woke up—wouldn't want to have
that talk.

We went to the meadow, every April, for decades
before we were caught
—and yes I should've known that second generation
deities can be contused
—and I chose that meadow when Hades came to me
or, rather, the closest
to those bright flowers my shimmering girl could come
under her mother's newest rule.
Olympians must only war by proxy lest Demeter muster

harvesters & beetles
to have her girl her way, and she's always feared the dead
I tried to save
Persephone from roses and bars. I almost got away with it,
& I know
she wanted to swallow her uncle's seeds. I know she knew
what seeds were
because I pulled apart her petals every time we went
to grass
and showed her all the parts . . . and what they could become

PERSEPHONE'S CANTO VIII

so this is marriage
once the white melts brown
narcissus down
he wakes up in green garters I didn't know
he owned
and whatever thrill I felt in his arm against my throat
is faded
when he takes elastic from his arm, his pink
sleeve limp
against the bicep that lifted me from grassland
by loaded
volcano where I never meant to stay

I'd stay
there now and never want
petals
or magma, or <!---there is no damage here--->

HERA'S CANTO

she'd cast about for other gods, demis, even men
while still pinned
into pinafore and bloomers—Demeter would've needed
all of Argus' eyes
to prevent that—and you know I never share if I can help it

like every girl, she wanted
the gentle hand, or at least a hand that could go soft,
respect
her needs—those males saw
her lace,
her pigtail braids; good ones, they did not believe
she was ready
she'd never be ready if she stayed with her mother
she wanted to be

so who was left but Hades, his fire and his horns?
she had to be burned
she didn't want it really but other ways
were gone

PERSEPHONE'S CANTO IX

uncle dad,
there's swimming here amongst the dead
& safer
than your oceans ever were—there are no tentacles
or sea lice
—damn, those hatchlings itch
maybe more
on skin frozen smooth by immortality
& overprotective
mother replaced by husbands who saves
me from youth & radiation
—sulfur white
-ns the spring in which I stretch and glide—
you'd be proud
of how smooth my strokes have become
though I've no way
of measuring my times down here—
I hear
mortals bathe in this kind of pool
for their skin,
but the heat exhausts them

having
a wonderful time,
love,
<rend="cursive">Perse</rend>

POSEIDON'S CANTO I

<damageSpan desc="water stained">
who among her uncles would not have fought our shadow
-brother for her
to carry her off? my chariot glints with suncapped waves
his with shadows
snakes of tongues roll growls and yelps in mouths of beasts
I will not call them dogs
that drag his hearse and I have dolphins
whales   sharks
if I need them and of course sea horses who could carry for her
whatever I made
in her—I mean I could have taken him and would never
have needed to fool
dear sweet Kore into swallowing pearls, she'd take my
milfoil
seeds to press between her plump
palms
and blow on them before quaffing them
with salt

before I was Uncle Sea and step-guardian of girls who tried to make her
keep her knees clean
she called me father, and her daddy Zeus gave her
up to Corpselord
and if those girls had run a little faster, risking grass stains on bleach, I'd have brought
my pitchfork
despite my brother-lord's decree </damageSpan>

PERSEPHONE'S CANTO X

when I am old I will wear
bruises
still inside my eyes, will wrinkle
not from sun
but from the damp down here
it makes
stalagmites and their tighter overhead
cousins meet
what is the word for nephews & nieces
& uncles & aunts
were not made to be collective, a grumble
of lights
and a herd of broken-winged swans
trumpeting
wilderness among the calcite columns
I am stone
-crumpled paper, a tea
-rinse
drama queen, like mother always said
I wanted
this, his flayed hands to lend
my pallor
red and blue so when I am old I can wear
violet
without the rainbow or the ultra
or the end

HEKATE'S CANTO I

like a bullfrog's throat an erratic
granite
crushed in mid-croak or a hundred thousand decades & thrones
of cicadas
gathered at the geyser's mouth at the wrong, reliable instant,
like the lodgepole pines
cracking all at once beneath Mt St Helens' lahars
I told Demeter
Event.observe(her daughter screamed, but I remember being such a <code>queen(){

blood-bloated
purple hands, closing on my neck, my screams
all animal
were not all death or <damage /></ code>

Intermezzo I: Clearing up the Question of Persephone's Consent

<ol>
<li>Either Persephone consented, or she did not.</li>
<li>If Persephone did not consent, she either withheld consent or was not capable of giving it.</li>
<li>If Persephone was not capable of giving consent, her inability was either caused by Hades, or it was not.</li>
<li>If Hades was the cause, either the pomegranate was fermented, or he terrified her.</li>
<li>If Hades so terrified Persephone that she could not refuse, either he intended to, or he did not.</li>
<li>If Hades intended to terrify Persephone, either he will admit it, or he will not.</li>
<li>If Hades will not admit that he intended to terrify Persephone, then either he is lying or he is not.</li>
<li>If Hades is not lying, then he will either tell us that he loves her or that he does not.</li>
<li>If Hades tells us he does not love her, then Persephone either will hear him, or will not.</li>
<li>If Persephone hears Hades, either she will interrupt him, or she will not.</li>
<li>If Persephone does not interrupt Hades, either we will call her later to hear her side, or we will not.</li>
<li>If we call her later to hear her side, either she will sit on her grave throne with a cool compress on her eyes and beg someone else to answer, or she will not.</li>
<li>If Persephone sits on her grave throne with a cool compress on her eyes and begs someone else to answer, either one of her shady acolytes will pick up the phone, or none of them will.</li>
<li>If none of them answer the phone, either we will ask the police to conduct a welfare check, or we will not.</li>
<li>If we ask the police to conduct a welfare check, they either will or will not.</li>
<li>If they conduct a welfare check, either they will find her among the dead, or they will not.</li>
<li>If the police do not find her, either we will be asked to come downtown to answer questions about Persephone's marriage, or we will not.</li>
<li>If we are asked to come downtown to answer questions about Persephone's marriage, we will say either Persephone consented or she did not.</li>
</ol>

HADES' CANTO I

I almost got away with it—my brother thought
he planned
my abduction of his daughter-niece who otherwise would know
no touch
of man, nor any yellow seed—a sealed
bud
in her mother's fields of muted gold—and that girl believes
she wanted me,
and for all I know she did, and the bucks and the bites that were all
her strength
were no more than passion. I got away with
more.
I'll never grow tired of my queen. When the shadows
of her eyes
begin to bore, and the way she sets the spirits to compete against their empty selves
grates,
then down comes Hermes to take her to see her mother who will never
visit my ice.
It's the perfect marriage, as ministers of Locri
know to brides who seek
Proserpina's benediction—for power when they're carried off
is only to survive,
and they must learn not to covet escape
from their cycles
and their own grim lords. Proserpina's never more lovely than when her eyes
carry sun
glints from above that narrow beneath me. Her fear is always
young.
I got away with more.

PERSEPHONE'S CANTO XI

the ribbon-tongues of serpent-flame that flash so thin
from yellow
clusters of burning anthers and filaments could never
be petals
—so much duller are their colors than even the ox
-eye daisy's
but they spiral and twist, and fertilize each other to heights—
here, depths
—no fleeing nymph nor tree born tree would dare to reach,
and roots
spread beyond what leaves can—weaving themselves into themselves
as shades
eventually do—what awe down here
to rule,
and I am of my marble throne, my eyes a color
-lessness
beyond gray, imperious, a joy
beyond joy
it is to be the Queen of Death

    ribbon   s of serpent-flame   flash
   yellow
        burning anthers and filaments   never
  petals
       duller   colors than   the ox
-eye daisy's
     spiral   twist, and fertilize
   depths
 no   born tree would   reach
and root
    beyond   leaves —weaving
  shades
     —what awe down here

to rule
          my marble throne, my eyes

beyond gray,
beyond joy
    to be the Queen of Death

                serpent-flame   flash
    yellow
        burn   anthers and filaments   never
  petal
                  colors   ox
-eye daisy's
              twist, and fertilize
    depths
  no   tree would   reach
and root
     beyond   weaving
   shades
        −what awe
to rule
        my   throne, my eyes

beyond
beyond joy
      the Queen of Death

              serpent   flash
   yellow
      burn   anthers and filaments   never
                colors
       twist,   fertilize

    depths
no   tree

      beyond
  shades
          what awe
to rule
                 my eyes

beyond
beyond
    the Queen of Death

          serpent

     burn   anthers and filaments

        twist   fertilize
  depths
no   tree

    beyond

        awe
 rule
               my eyes

beyond
beyond
    the Queen   Death

                    serpent

                    anthers   filaments

                  twist   fertilize
  depths

      beyond

                    awe

                          my eyes

beyond
beyond
             Queen   Death

                    serpent

                    anthers

                  twist   fertilize
  depths

      beyond

                            eyes

beyond
beyond
        Queen   Death

      serpent

      anthers

      twist   fertilize
depths

  beyond

beyond
beyond
         Death

      serpent

      twist
depths

  beyond

                        Death

                    twist
depths

    beyond

                        Death

                    twist

depths

            Death

depth

            Death

Death

HADES' CANTO II

because she pulled flowers up by their petals & twisted off their heads
because it never snowed
because I could already see how my hell's gray would purify her gold-black hair
because she was too young
because her father agreed: she ought to be touched
because she screamed
because when she stopped screaming, she moaned

because she needs it
because she lets the sun disrupt the ashes of her eyes
because her sunlight fades
because she only listens when my hands press at her throat
because she loves her mother
because she fears her mother enough to choose my seeds
because she swallows for me
because the living believe she offers them a better deal when they die
because she lusts to torture them more than I
because she leaves
because whatever seeds I plant in her, even ground-up glass, she will make bear fruit
because the river froze
because her Seahawks smashed my 'Niners again
because she forgets that she said no
because she traces shattered glass into my back if I let her arms go free
because I'm as dead as I'm immortal
because she knew what I was when she tore the red skin to drink me and stay
because she'll write about it
because what else was a goddess of the growing & wilting vine made to take
because she is mine

my pussy
        my breasts
                my grime-streaked towel around her wrists
because her lips
will grey

PERSEPHONE'S CANTO XII

sometimes I burn
in the sun I forget what I want
to get away

and those are the years Hades erupts
armored,
without chariot, his pale body rises in red until he catches
arm or hem
and pulls me to his chest until he grasps
my breasts
remember, he says, you don't have to do this
I nod—he pinches
my nipple, I swallowed the seeds <del rend="stroked">, and if I said no
would he
let me stay here and serve and starve for a touch
that isn't woven
to whip,</del> and there are heavier whips in hell
between soft
-er strokes, and what is he asking—consent, he says, you don't
oh yes
his hand's already in my coarser hair
yes,
and the lava inches us down, pressing us closer as it becomes
magma
and I burn with slowness   of our descent
& he ties
me to no marble slab but a gray
air mattress
he pins my eyes open, says he wants to watch the sunlight
fade
I have to watch his teeth becoming fangs
breaking
me, he smears me in my blood <damageSpan desc="stain">

my body \</damageSpan\>
quivers in its new flamepaint, but I can't buck, or twist
beneath his knots
and then there's his \<unclear\>body\</unclear\>, pressing into pressing
until I give

and neither heat nor dark can touch
what's gone

HADES' CANTO II

dead women can't say no, and she's
divine
so why she stopped after her first time
even her daddy
couldn't say—guess my hell's just blessed that way—
her shoulder bending
under my knees, her lips stretching to take me in whole
she bruises
so easy and thanks me for rising and thanks me for roses
blooming in her skin
in purples and puces her mother and will never know

PERSEPHONE'S CANTO XIII

when he came for me, I screamed—Athena or the neat
-ankled Oceanids will tell you
—but so many things are forgotten in hell, I thought I could add my
no

—strut you peacocks, strut as if all your eyes were not dead
in my house
where paralyzed showers of dust, unpierced by sun
rays,
will cover you as your reward once you've learned to cease
moving like the living
as I have learned to still my arms that cannot lift my grim
god's body from mine

—oh give me my dust, you seething walls of soil
forget
how I put all my motion in my hips—I'll still my
desire, too

I almost got away with it
almost changed
my history of no to yes I will yes lord yes yes yes
but I'm harder
than marble these days and hold my memories
clearer than stones
hold their epitaphs: here lies Kore
's pit

and still I'll root down here, with Hades
& packed
sod instead of sky to feed my leaves—my fruit
will be mildewed garnets
—for what's above but fists of wheat, and daddy who becomes a bird or bull

to rape
so I'll become the tree of hell, watered
by Styx,
running my juices down throats of my initiates:
intoxicated shades

are all I will know, and all will know me

by power I stole
from the grim lord who stole me

HADES' CANTO III

Persephone is eating pomegranates in the dark
each night   she refuses
the will o' wisp of the sulfur bog, and the soul-diffused
red light
of the magmatic moor. She skulks beside basalt
columns without
calcium salts. Of all the women I've dragged down here
only she consumes
bitterness—the white membrane—I've offered
my knife
for her to pop the rotten garnets right out.

I fear her now
and the thin wilderness of her scent so unlike
her mother

Intermezzo II: Letters of Support

Dear Proserpina,

I, too, almost got away
with eating wicked fruit,
but I had Nobodaddy
and a husband
instead of Daddy Zeus
and Mother Wheat.

They wouldn't give me half
the year for my beloved
serpent to crush
my bones & lungs in his embrace.

You are married to your snake.
Adam, whose I am, connived
with God. He ate the fig
and they pretended
it was the same damn sin,
and Yahweh banished us
to a world without Hell
's exciting torments.

Enjoy the freezing fireworks
that burn inside your eyelids,
Proserpina, on my behalf.

Love,
Eve

Dear Despoina,

the wives and mothers
of monsters meet
by the river at three

Love,
Lilith

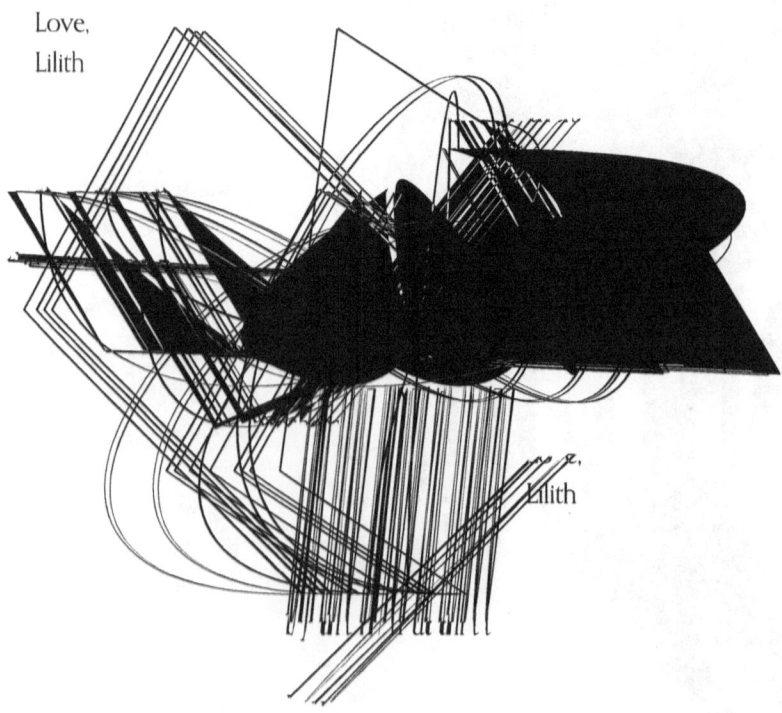

Dear Melinoia,

You will find yourself becoming awful. Cradle
that awe to the side of your sternum, in the rib-protect
-ed hole
that in mortals carries a heart. When someone you love
vomits and flees your visage and your hollowhung
skin
, that awe will keep you warm.

Yours,
Inanna

Dearestinplaces Proserpinsephondespoiamelidikiste cthonia, legisletter, misstriste, barer of pomegrapplefigrape:

Even in my tricklies, I flewed mamatains for mentowns, and you too sicklecycle so be low, be glow, be dazzle, be whys to his zeds n zorries, and members the big mans never sos big as hell say he is, fear not, as I told my onliest Iss (whists Proserpronette drips peas from her slit
satchel), drink up the dregs, you might as well love him when all's said and did, don't be a sacralfice, don't be a stone, nor even of loam, go for the potion, be he Triste am be he March, and some years you'll be back to your source before 'im. All the wheat and gold is by the banks and bests and beats and breaths. Be glee, she.

Sinlovely,
All Living Plurabelle

Dearest of Chthonic Gods:

these men of shade
-d desires cleave
—that's all of them—
yours would bind my heart
to the restlessness of men

who think they fight for me
their blood is just a game
mud & bone the squares

I played against myself
in my time: love-lust
versus war-lust
and all about the body

I always won

and then your father split me up
and married me to a god
his wife broke

is it any wonder
I cheated with myself?
or that sometimes I curl in an
oyster,
make a pearl, and artists think
I was born of such a shell
but listen, Venus, wasn't always
about plastic & brands

I'm the reason her light rises
first & steadiest every dusk

when your mother's spy gives up—
Persephone, what I'm saying is, forget
them all: his needs, her wants,
forget that you said yes or no
be everything

I used to be

Yours in blood & love,
Ishtar

dear proserpine,

the womyn
you will already know
would rather buy his beer
than your black bush,
would rather feel their fingers
in his hair than soothe your braids

the men you'll find
will want to find
themselves inside the queen
of hell

    and bad girls get abandoned
when the taxi leaves
for the airport, when your brother bleeds
out after battle

do not take him   to your escape
to sleep
    no, not your dying lover
father, husband, uncle neither

love,
morgan le fay

ps i hope the necklace with the pink
beryl fits your neck
tightly

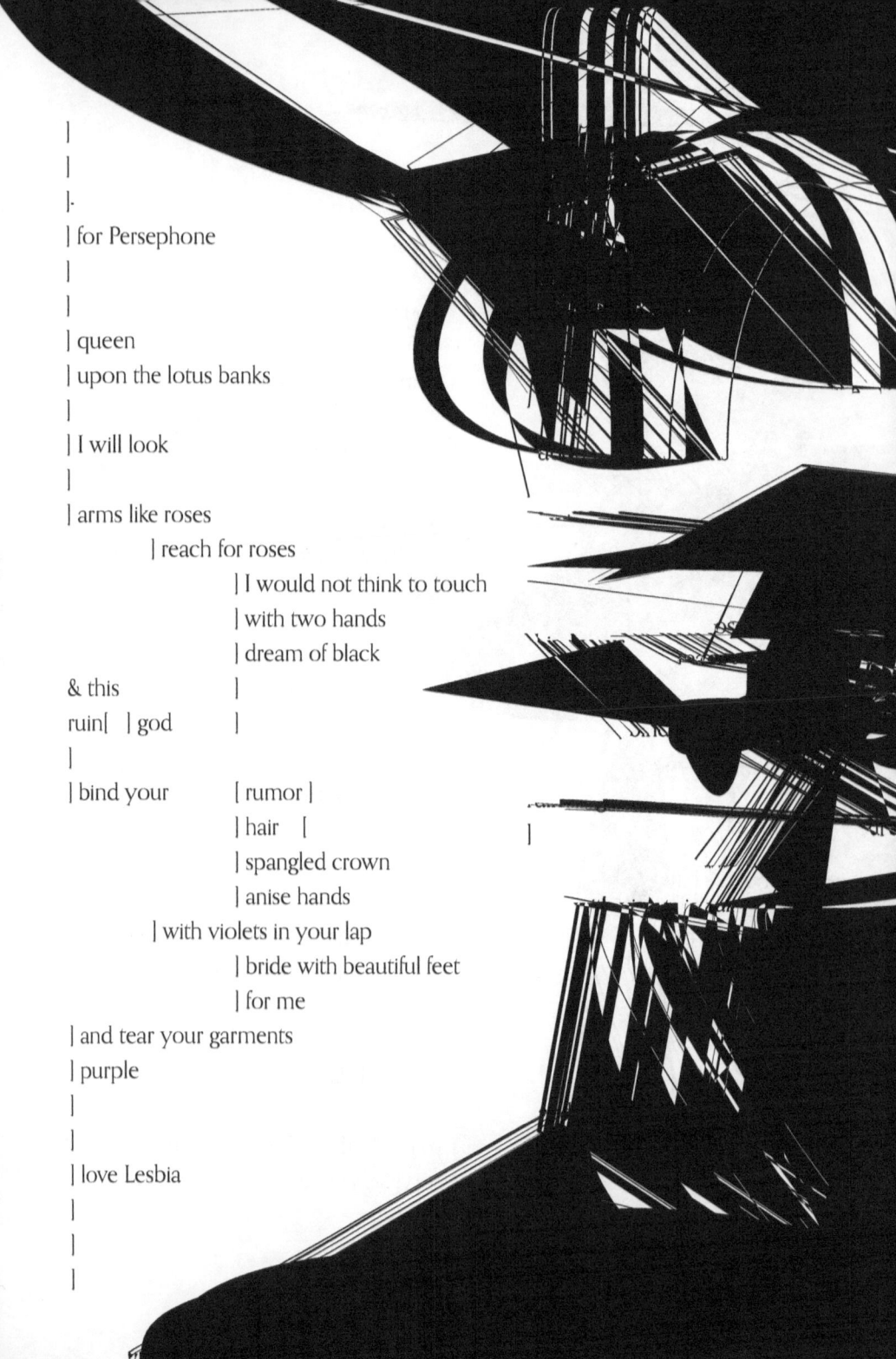

]
]
].
] for Persephone
]
]
] queen
] upon the lotus banks
]
] I will look
]
] arms like roses
      ] reach for roses
           ] I would not think to touch
           ] with two hands
           ] dream of black
& this   ]
ruin[ ] god   ]
]
] bind your   [rumor]
          ] hair [
          ] spangled crown
          ] anise hands
     ] with violets in your lap
        ] bride with beautiful feet
        ] for me
] and tear your garments
] purple
]
]
] love Lesbia
]
]
]

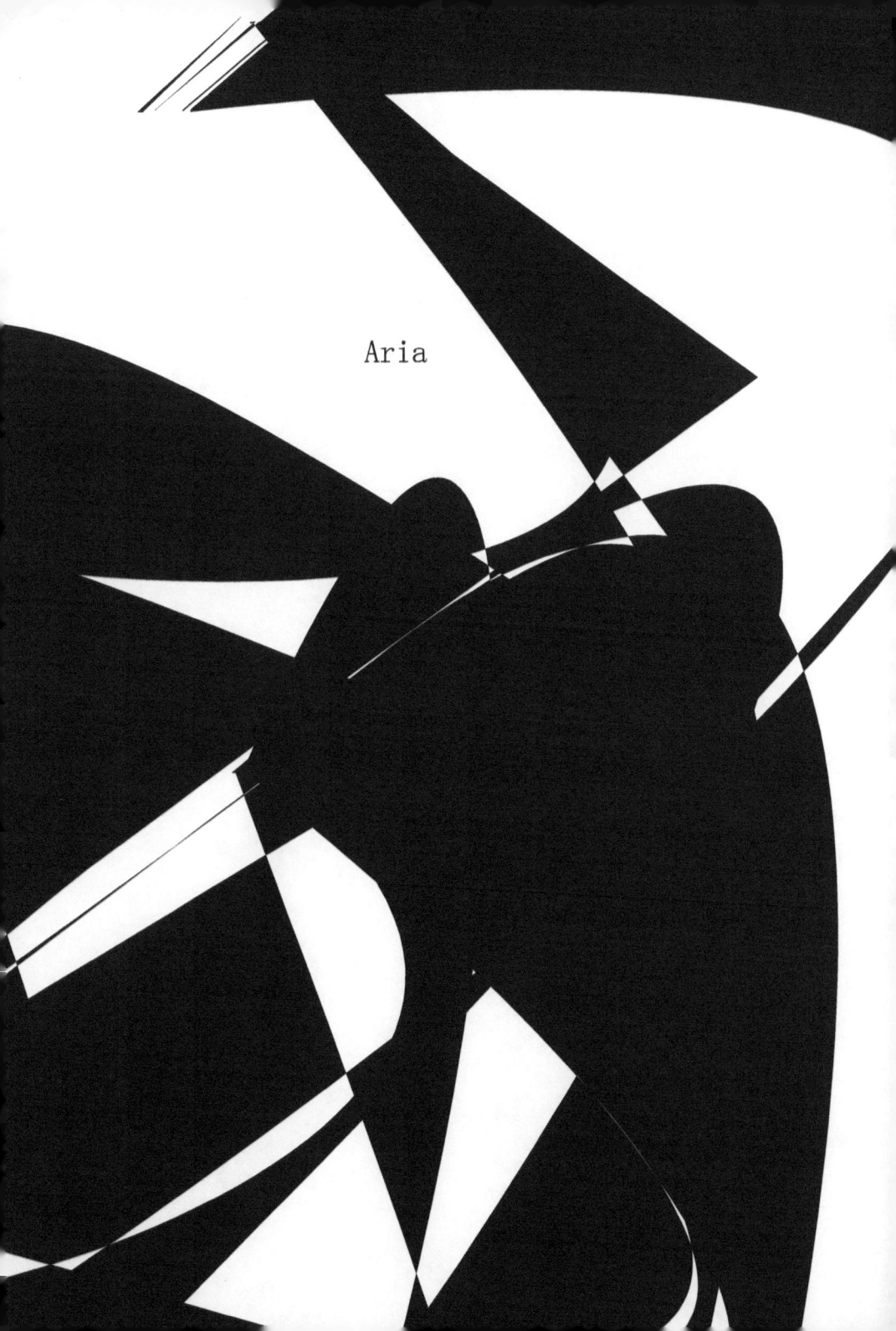

PERSEPHONE'S CANTO TO HELEN

come then, face,
and the rest of your shape, down to my no grayer palace
than you've haunted
since your savior-abductor wifed you again

all for you
my lord says your lord set fire to the sea—I say
it was for his heart,
for feasts among his fighting men where he'd sit nearest those who'd pierced
shield & bone,
initiates of the crunch above a woman's bloom with a bee still thrusting its way in—
Helen, hush,
you did none of this. You didn't even love Paris, except that cheap
trinket goddess
needed you to win another bauble for the shelf beside the urn
empty
of what she should have left of Adonis

come down to me
lovely one, and I will teach you to be feared, to carve your face
beyond beauty

come now, to me, Helen, though I give you a choice,
only if you obey
me will you ever be free of Menelaus and the war
we'll freeze
your tears in amber, your heart in salt

No, Helen
would not descend on her own feet but waited until flakes
of currency
covered her eyes. She would not rule
with me

—such is the sodality of stolen women who choose
to love
the lords of our bodies that have never been ours

PERSEPHONE'S CANTO TO PROMETHEUS

o exalted callus
-ed hands and wrists and scarless
shreds of skin
over the large, globed, glandular organ
that purifies,
think of me as your long-distance admirer
& eagle's beak
no arm of Hercules can save you
from serving

I will have you, and your foolish brother, together
to tea
—before you decline, remember that ghosts bring leaves
of green, black, white, red
that brew up steams the living can only dream
& forget
because they do not have the words to remember
taste & scent
the way we do beneath the loam and tips of roots
where dim
-ness fade all the senses of mortal and divine

and after tea, the mysteries
—such as how many ways the old, expired deities
can violate the children
of the new ruling class, and how my broken generation
can seize control
of Wall Street, Constitution, airplanes, cruise ships, limousines, stadia, and thrones

PERSEPHONE'S CANTO TO DEMOPHOON

she was always like that—throw your pink
skin in flames
and scream if you didn't recognize the gift
I can see
your chubby fearlessness, grasping for the smoke
laughing
at the red that lashed your cheeks, throwing
ash over shoulders
you could not yet name, and who would not scream
to see you burn,
and who would not scream more to see
that you did not?
she was always like that—why don't you know the price
of that blue pot
in sacrifice and slaves? why can't you paint it properly
around your eyes
every daughter knows how it's done, every mother
& nurse
should be able to see when a son's being made
immortal
she was always like that—and yet we scream more
in other arms

PERSEPHONE'S CANTO TO TYPHAON

your mother rots under command
of earth
and pregnant sun, bacteria and bugs
make earth
of her scales and sphincters
my mother
has fangs and yours was never venomous
just because she squeezed
men to redden her river, Apollo deemed her evil
and Hades
deems me wife because he dragged me down—
your mother
made the river flow <caesura /> is what the gods won't say
at least she felt
the piercing—my wounds give no blood to taste

and she
is not your mother, you belong
on Olympus
sure as I belong where sun can see
Hera birthed you
in revenge for wisdom coming through the head
of Zeus's cunt
but you are blessed, carrying to massacres
the memory of a loving
skin, caressing all around you—no, there are
no snakes in hell

PERSEPHONE'S CANTO TO DIONYSUS

when the men took you young
man of curled
sandy hair none of their bonds
could stay
around your wrists and ankles more
slender than mine
your slightness was your savior and the slick
-ness of your skin
eased you into panther's pelt so you could as a shadow
devour them

when I rise let's share a casket
of wine
and wrap every altar, mountain, tower, and sea
in ivy

PERSEPHONE'S CANTO TO HEPHAISTOS

come now, be kindly, Hephaistos—I'm easy
to teach
to mine the stones that obey without losing
shape & strength
for I am already low where I rule
close
to Gaia's most clotted veins

as you taught
cave-dwellers to craft eaves in their shelters,
indoctrinate me
to make the matters of the black earth say
what I desire
instead of what already is <damage />

PERSEPHONE'S CANTO TO EURYDICE

rage, yes
corpse that you are I've made you see
his kind
will always look behind to see that you are following
or any girl
seduced by lyre or guitar—three chords are usually enough—
I let you go
again back towards the world where all your Orpheuses
gaze
knowing you were doomed to slide back to my dim
kingdom knowing
you could not be loved any better in sunlight

I'd tell you you'll become
crocuses more sapphire than the sky, more golden than the sun
but you want no comfort
that cannot be seen among the laughing girls
who make hell burn

PERSEPHONE'S CANTO TO RED

you've been down here and called it
love
unrequited, adolescent, recalled
when wounds
could neither be seen nor ignored

blood
has its value it breaks out through the mud
of demimortal flesh
as tears, mother assures me, water something healthy

but do not break his grasp
or the foul god you thought you loved comes back
a warrior
who murdered you and your little dog, too
I've been gored
for less and ought to know

PERSEPHONE'S CANTO TO ADONAIS

none shall sanctify the flowers that spring
you
from the dead so long as lilies bleed
pure red
and call it my love above these roots and rotten
night-loam

each flame is named for a petal and given
to trumpet
bloom, to stamen, to bee, to flutter by
with mother-bird
hypnotized by the charm
bracelets
                         of Aphrodite

PERSEPHONE'S CANTO TO ELEKTRA

you should have stayed in her
red
and purple and dark
rock rose
robes and stayed in her way to open
porticoes
there never was a temple; the rhod
-odendron has
no deity but bees who crawl into her horn
before the curse
made you a murderess, you could

have stung
all the same, Aegean sea beats waves
against salt waves
and you will never turn to foam, like me
you'd never give
your legs away as though love is love and real

my hair
you've dreamt around the warm
fat
of your fingers, my fingers you've breathed
colder
than marble or a corpse still called a corpse
into your lower hair
and Agamemnon said I was a woman with a wheat-spike head
and like a maiden
you said nothing; you are not mine, Elektra

but your brother's
and my grim lord's to be

PERSEPHONE'S CANTO TO NARCISSUS

you died for my flower, my suck
-ing bulb,
my lure, allure of the horned god's road
a daffodil, a shallow
orange bowl among white petals you'd call fair
as your skin
or mine as Death saw it then, but now we are more pale
than white
in this narkissos, this numbness, I brought the flower
down with me

it does not wilt, though Echo pined, and I have nearly had my fill
of feeling
nothing, of doing my lord god's will

"draperies of stone" "the black / velvet ribbon" "her uniform printed with flowers" "berries of the m
and bubbling" "pawed over by scholars" "in a pair of red Keds" "drowning in flowers" "[m]ixing and
Tampax tubes" "golden poppies" "lemony amber"
"the meadow without the daisies" "a small / green flame" "part the green sheathes" "green tresses"
"wood" "blue-veined breasts" "blue people in blue houses / under blue trees" "blue, blue everywh
white fire
bloom sticks" "incinerated" "there are no laws" "his watch, / his wrist" "the writhing, bronze ribbon"

"you spurn / your petulant colors" "and you are sinking" "slippery avenue of stone" "smeared with
bowl / in the earth" "just stirring the darkness" "on the white / path"

Intermezzo III: In Other Words

sh" "did she cooperate in her rape" "stained with red juice" "with the blood of the world" "foaming
/ I felt the earth" "the sour ecstasy of bread" "to let the garden go to seed" "rotten fruit and

ve" "green oblivion" "buil[t] with" "bones" "your basic sunshine pouring through" "blue and blood
avy blue sweater" "an indigo scarf" "that vintage / purple lace" "bodies bloom and burn" "sapped
/ dissolving" "exactly where pink turns into white" "a pearl, or a parasite" "a pail of milk" "a pyre of

sh" "the father's bedclothes" "[a]nd always you ask" "father, brother, or lover" "uplifted / arms" "a

Fragments in this section come from Rita Dove's *Mother Love*, Louise Glück's *Averno*, Lyn Lifshin's *Persephone*, John Most's *Persephone* (by Hannah Nijinsky), and Alison Townsend's *Persephone in America*.

PERSEPHONE'S CANTO XXV

</daughter>
</hell>

POSEIDON'S CANTO II

. . . and she has ordered dimmed cities of living bone
to build themselves
in my realm, to kill themselves to fossilize
rings
of islands against the breakers I should send
but will not

I'd have taken her with her daddy's leave
& I should've been
her father, instead of giving up her mother
's womb
to the power of my little brother
who shocks
everything I carry inside when he turns
sky
white on white over my waves—and when she
grows worlds
within me, then that's as good as anything
I could've done

with Hades' liberties—towers of antlers
& yellow
crinkled rounds, as if her brain were in my body, and fractal
blue spires

so rooted to the hell that's beneath me, too, I couldn't
wash them away
even if I wanted to—what else could she do
to interrupt
my currents and re-direct my sharks?

the queen of hell
should not be able to breathe where red

light can't reach
her salt-sopped hair, her glistening cheeks

PERSEPHONE'S CANTO XXVI

. . . and I've made a Heaven out of Hell
's heat
and man will make his hells out here, splitting
atoms,
splitting sovereign hairs and aid to fix
his sewers
turning islands into sea-wolf sleeping grounds,
and I'll still be
under the pandanus tree's twisted rootwork
while dragonflies press
thoraxes together and spin their single-layer flesh
wings
in my eternal sunlight—butterflies belong
to mother,
painted like she made me paint my eyes
I've sworn
them all to silence with the fruit that looks
like jellyfish
when it falls; noni's seeds are in its substance
& it binds
no one to anything but bodies </caesura > where they already live

DEMETER'S CANTO II

. . . and somehow I can't find this place
the tropics
with their heat from hell, however I sulk
& weep
despite what my brothers have said, I'm certain
it's Hades' plot

and even he cannot hide any place on earth from me
forever
and I will continue to round and round
the marble
bringing spring with me so the places I am not
shiver & starve
until I find my daughter and an arm or ear or toe
for trawling her home
through lava or salt to the hermitage where she will learn
to sit & watch

PERSEPHONE'S CANTO XXVII

. . . and I know tide pools
where moon
snails suck the marrow from bones
they've pierced,
and the marrow is life when your skeleton
's outside

the bivalves I watched die before I went
down to death
derive their name from bond, a bondage
& limped
their links to dark volcanic remnants

rock beach here
is lighter, pressed with outlines of spiral shells
there is still predation
I have not forgiven him; I see these souls
already were with him
if such a silent, shy creature, as I once was
can be called a so . . .

ARTEMIS'S CANTO II

. . . and she still loves lushness—look how green
palms & bōb
, on stilted roots and twisted spine, grow—
she gathers purple
urchin spines from pools in the dead, brown coral—
shadows of shells
that never sent what they contained
to sulfur & flame—
limestone is a sedimentary rock, made mostly of dolomite or calcium carbonate—

she is alone
without volcanoes since she divorced him—
though he filed
under the indigo gilded dome of Olympus
and Charon rose
and poled his ferry through the Panama Canal,
across a couple oceans,
for her signature when the court finally acted—

she is alone
most days, leaving the infant none of us have seen
unswaddled
with some local mermaid—not a god's daughter, a mistress
of the Arno School
of lovemaking, who has held so many young girls' hands
as they floated
to feel the waves beneath them and learn to give
good undulation,
and who would not hide or giggle if Hades
tried to exercise
paternal rights <caesura /> the mermaid's teeth
are yellow

and Persephone now could join my band, except she has
her own niche
                    and prey

PERSEPHONE'S CANTO XXVIII

of course I love the buttressed pines
mini-palms
more like in leaves, their fruits
leave
fibers stretched between my teeth and taste like
nothing
we had in Greece or Italy or Hell—almost
citrus
carrot—but not quite—but I
don't love now
the pouring and the steam of summer without husband
or mother to take me

sometimes broader palm leaves fall—real palms and coconuts and I
caress
them up along my sides and stretch marks
& then I swim

      I call this life . . .

THE OCEANIDS' CANTO II

oh stop we want our islands too,
our screw
pines with green-tipped yellow fruit
to suck
between our pearl teeth—she leaves
oysters
to chew their gems, as if irritation were better
than death
and life in shell more precious than <!---there is no damage here--->

PERSEPHONE'S CANTO XXIX

electric sky
no longer only white on white
sliced
by father, lower down the port red mated
green
and followed forty paces back by flash
-ing white
that can't compare to lightning I once knew it was
inevitable
lights would one day reach their way up from rock
fringes of coral
across the waves: canoes found them, whaling
ships found them,
metal balloons knew where to land, and so do jets
at Kwajalein
with missiles under their wings like tumors
in armpits
it was inevitable that the bomb would be dropped
on me

other islands had to be evacuated, but the camouflage
men can't see
divinity, and whoever told you radiation glows
green lied
the yams now match my wine
-dark flush
on cheeks as pale as ever I was
with Hades
my love

HADES' LAST CANTO

. . . and she'll come back
when Demeter has found her, or when she finds the coral
horns
don't do it for her like mine did; she can take those con
-joined polyps down
her throat, but rooted to the sea floor, they
can't force her
and she loves to use the husky voice
that lingers
after that job—I want her green—she'll come

back green
as she was in the meadow she de
-flowered herself
—and it won't be better willing, but my liquid
highway petrifies
when it meets the sea, and limestone has no passages
for my heat & me

even if the sky is always lava as the sun
collapses
into breakers—if postcards can be believed
she will come back to me

PERSEPHONE'S CANTO XXX

I float
and if I kick, it is without
heading
I have no sense of north and south
living
in a circle will do that to a girl
who used to know
which way each corpse was buried
facing

what happened underground
is impossible
on an atoll because I wish it so
and I'm alone
in my divinity from reef
to reef

HEKATE'S CANTO II

you will not shine anymore
I'm sure
someone has told you that
I'm sure
it hardly matters as
I'm sure
we do not know the consequence
of your divorce
if only, child, I knew <unclear reason="tear" />

PERSEPHONE'S LAST CANTO

... and I will not go back to hell
it was not I
who swallowed his seeds, who turned them red, for I
know how to damn
and pardon, too, and how to twist torment inside of clemency
—witness, Orpheus—
I am the wicked queen who eats the virginal thing's
heart & cunt

to save her: girls who've never known winter
wilt
under the men, the gods who suckle on deep dead roots
of oaks
with stumps already fed to secondary growth—
they have mothers
who would give them everything, but they still want us—

it was not I
who swallowed his seeds: it was such a girl:
pale lips,
hair pure of ash, no freckles, and just her first
rock-rose bruise

she brought winter into the world—not the girl,
the mother,
—everyone confuses them on phone—
and I will not
go back to her, to hell, to her, to hell, to mother, whatever he was

coral
will be the ring beneath my feet—no more fire, no more
basalt
though polyps have built on hell as much as I

will not go back
these tropical atolls will always have the heat
that I have lifted
from the realm of the grim lord I
was not the one
who convinced myself to call my lord, my husband,
lover
, god, divine—if there is salt, let it be said it belongs
to Oceanus
and if there is humidity, let it be the price
of eternal summer

these are not my tears—it was not I who let
him lift my lips apart
and put his glistening seeds inside

& yet this child is mine

to raise in names her people will teach me to pronounce

──────── **ABOUT THE AUTHOR** ────────

Elizabeth Kate Switaj is an academic administrator and cat rescuer in the Republic of the Marshall Islands. She holds a PhD from Queen's University Belfast and an MFA from New College of California. Her first collection of poetry, Magdalence & the Mermaids, was published by Paper Kite Press in 2009 and her book of literary criticism, James Joyce's Teaching Life and Methods was published by Palgrave Macmillan in 2016. She previously taught in Japan and China and has been diving with bull sharks, whale sharks, and manta rays.

11:11 Press is an American independent literary publisher based in Minneapolis, MN. Founded in 2018, 11:11 publishes innovative literature of all forms and varieties. We believe in the freedom of artistic expression, the realization of creative potential, and the transcendental power of stories.

www.ingramcontent.com/pod-product-compliance
Lightning Source LLC
Chambersburg PA
CBHW022008120526
44592CB00034B/748